DAILY BIBLE DEVOTIONAL FOR COUPLES

5-Minutes devotion to grow in faith and joy

Ronnie D. Kissner

DAILY BIBLE DEVOTIONAL FOR COUPLES

5-Minutes devotion to grow in faith and joy

Ronnie D. Kissner

Table of Content

Week 1

Sunday

Topic : God wants a joyous heart
Text : Psalm 69:30-32

Inspiration

How do I praise God? God doesn't want an animal sacrifice, he wants a sacrifice of the heart. He wants a joyous heart, a heart that bursts into song because it can't help itself. A heart so full of gratitude that song is the only way a body can express it. I love music; I love to sing the songs of praise in church. I might not have the best voice but it's the one God gave me so he must think it's good enough. There is something about music that lifts the soul. It's no wonder that the psalms are music. In fact, this psalm even tells us which piece of music to sing it to – "Lilies!" When we think about it, some of the most glorious music was written for religious reasons: Handel's Messiah is but one example. When we listen to the anthems of many nations, we see how they give thanks and praise to God. Whether we raise our voices in song or not, what is important is that we raise our voices in thanks and praise to God. Our prayers acknowledge that we know who is in charge, to whom we owe everything and who deserves our praise.

Prayer

Loving God, you have given us everything we have and you deserve out thanks and praise, may we raise our voice daily to your name. Amen.

Note   Date:

_____

_____

_____

_____

_____

_____

_____

_____

_____

Monday

Topic : Go and tell them
Text : John 1:41-41

Inspiration

The first thing Andrew did when He found out
Jesus Christ was to go tell his brother. Andrew went
and got Peter and brought him to Jesus.He first
findeth his own brother Simon, and saith unto him,
We have found the Messias, which is, being
interpreted, the Christ. And he brought him to
Jesus. And when Jesus beheld him, he said, Thou
art Simon the son of Jona: thou shalt be called
Cephas, which is by interpretation, A stone.
Andrew could have been scoffed at or rejected by
Peter if Peter did not believe Jesus was the Christ;
yet, Andrew took him to Jesus anyways, and I'm
sure he was glad he did. You have Jesus, and you
love Him. Have you tried to bring your family to
Him? Knowing Jesus is the only way to eternal life,
wouldn't you want to try your best to introduce Him
to your grandparents, mother, father, brothers,
sisters, and cousins?

Prayer

Heavenly Father, give me strength and courage to introduce You to my family. They need You. I want to speak to them about You. Help me to tell them about You well. Help me to answer questions they have and to try to find them the answers I don't know. Soften their hearts. Only You can bring them to You, so please do so. In Jesus' name. Amen.

Note   Date:

_____

_____

_____

_____

_____

_____

_____

_____

_____

Tuesday

Topic : Doing what Jesus tells us to do
Text : Luke 10:41-42

And Jesus answered and said unto her, Martha,
Martha, thou art careful and troubled about many
things:
But one thing is needful: and Mary hath chosen that
good part, which shall not be taken away from her.

Inspiration

  In today's gospel, Martha is busy about hospitality
and Mary extends hospitality in a quieter manner.
We need both, and we need to be both. There are
times when we need to be about doing what Jesus
tells us to do, but if all we do is "do" and we don't
take the time to listen, we just might get it wrong.
Mary sits and listens to Jesus while Martha feels
overwhelmed with her tasks. When Martha
complains, Jesus tells her not to be anxious and
worried, and I think that here is the key. When we
take the time to sit and listen to Jesus and then
move on to follow the will of God, we don't have to
be anxious and worried; we can relax in the
knowledge that we are doing our best, and that is
what is required of us. Jesus doesn't say that what

Martha is doing is unimportant; he just seems to imply that she shouldn't be so focused on her work, that she neglects her need for being present and listening. We, too, can be so busy doing that we forget to take the time to pray, to reflect on Scripture, to sit and listen to Jesus. During the sometimes lazy days of summer, let us take advantage of the laziness and just sit in God's presence and reflect on who we are and who we are called to be, so that when the time comes to be busy again, we'll be ready.

Prayer

Gracious God, you want us to be hospitable and welcoming to all but you also want us to know that listening to you and learning from you is also important. Let us never be so busy that we forget to take time to spend with you. Amen.

Note   Date:

_____

_____

_____

_____

_____

_____

_____

_____

_____

Wednesday

Topic : Work for justice if you want peace
Text : Micah 2:1-2

Inspiration

Micah is a prophet at around the same time as Isaiah and has come to prophesy punishment to those who are behaving in an unjust manner. Just because a person has the power or authority to act unjustly, doesn't mean that he should. One might think that harassment or schemes to defraud people of their property or their inheritance, are something new, but Micah lets us know that these things have been going on since antiquity. God isn't any happier today about these practices than he was then. Micah made known God's displeasure to the kings and leaders of the day. He warns that their unjust practices need to stop and that the people need to repent or else they are leaving themselves open to attack by armies greater than theirs.

As we know, Assyria and Babylon both decimated Judah and Israel. Think about the Roman Empire, they too had fallen into such a moral decay that they were open to being overcome by Constantine. What about today? We have become lax in our time as well. Corporate takeovers that have little respect for the rights of the workers have become common. Even companies that have not been taken over have been known to change their policies and limit the benefits that their employees enjoy. Communities can take property away from individuals for schools, highways, shopping centers, by eminent domain and those who live on the properties are forced to move. Although owners are reimbursed, renters need to fend for themselves. Looking out for number one, whether personally, communally or nationally can lead to ignoring the essentials and there is nothing to stop others from overcoming us. As Micah says, we need to work for justice if we want peace.

Note   **Date:**

_____

_____

_____

_____

_____

_____

_____

_____

Thursday

Topic : The name of God
Text : Exodus 3:13-14

Inspiration

God's name as it is written in Scripture is either
Jehovah or Yahweh, or just YHWH. All are
translations of He is Who He is. Because the Jewish
people did not call God by the name he gave Moses.
It is for this reason that the Jewish people were so
angry when Jesus said that before Abraham came
to be I AM. To say God's name was to blaspheme.
For the people of Moses' time, names had power.
They felt that to use the name of God was to say
that they had power over God, and so the name was
sacred. I can remember an uncle of mine who
would often take not just the Lord's name in vain
when he was angry, but would also use it to curse
whoever he was angry with. I'm sure you know
many people who do the same without even
blinking an eye.

Good Christians, all, who would be horrified if they
were called on it. We are offended when people use
foul language, why are we not offended when the
Lord's name is taken in vain? A friend of mine used

to work in the office of a major manufacturing company and the man who sat behind her was continually cursing the company and its managers. One day she had had enough and turned to him and said, "No wonder the company is going to pot, you keep asking God to damn it." He had never considered that he was both swearing and cursing, but he stopped. What about us? Do we need to clean up our speech, or ask other to do so?

Prayer

 Lord, your commandments ask us to not swear or curse, to not take your name in vain and yet we hear this commandment being ignored all the time. Help us to keep your name and sacred and to ask others to do so as well. Amen.

Note   Date:

Friday

Topic: God hears us
Text : Exodus 3:9-10

Inspiration

 God hears us. He hears the cries of his people when
they are being oppressed. In this case, the people of
Israel were being oppressed by the Egyptians and
God had placed Moses in a position to help them be
free. God hears his people cry today. There is
oppression in some countries of Christians and also
of the Jews. God never abandoned his chosen
people, and he doesn't abandon those who have
chosen to follow his Son, Jesus. Sometimes
oppression occurs in the workplace or
neighborhoods as well. Men and women can be
oppressed because of religious beliefs, for race, for
language, for country of origin, for economic status,
or for gender. While I was still in college a friend
got a job teaching in an inner city school. Because
the children were mostly from poor families and
minorities, the budget for supplies was not the
same as that for schools in better neighborhoods.
People got together and demanded equality. It took
time, but God guided them to victory. We have a
responsibility to be available for God to use to help

free people from oppression. Sometimes it is standing up for equality in the workplace, sometimes it is working for non-discrimination in our policies providing access to a good education for all students. We also have a responsibility to pray for freedom of religion in the world. God is Father to all creation, and he doesn't want any of his creatures to suffer oppression. We need to make sure that we are part of the solution, not part of the problem because of our own possible prejudices.

Prayer

Lord and father of us all, may we never be oppressors of your children; may we keep our eyes open and our ears also to hear the cries of those who suffer and do what we can for them. Amen.

Note   Date:

_____

_____

_____

_____

_____

_____

_____

_____

_____

Saturday

Topic : Love of God should come first
Text : 1Corinthians 15:12-14

Inspiration

 Doubt is normal. It was there in Paul's time and it
exists today. Maybe it is more prevalent today than
it was in Paul's time because there are so many
people trying to discourage people from belief in
God. The pagans of Paul's time believed in gods,
they just didn't all know God. Today many claim
that there is no God. They believe that scientists will
soon be able to explain everything about how the
world was created and answer any other question
we might have. See, no need for God! And if there is
no God then no heaven and no resurrection. If this
is true then why bother depriving ourselves of all
the pleasures we can get just because Christianity
says love of God and of others should come first.
But, there were too many people who witnessed
Jesus after his resurrection. Too many people who
were willing to die for the sake of Jesus and his
teaching. I don't know about you, but I wouldn't die
for a lie. And I doubt that they would either. So, as
Paul says, since Jesus rose from the dead, we need
to pay attention to what he said and to the promise

that one day we too would rise if only we remain faithful. Doubt? Okay, but in the end, trust and belief.

Prayer

Dear God, we believe that you have sent your son into the world to fulfill the promise of salvation. We trust in you inspite of those who would try to turn us away from you. We do believe, help our unbelief. Amen.

Note   Date:

Week 2

Sunday

Topic : Put God first
Text : Matthew 10:34-36

Inspiration

We are called on to make choices all the time. We can choose God, or we can choose other. Is that late night party worth missing church? We can talk all we want about being too busy, but the truth is that we find the time for what we want to do. I love to read, knit, spend time with my friends and I hate doing the laundry, dishes, vacuuming, but it all needs to be done. I would rather pick up a good book than exercise. I can say that I am "too busy" to do the things I don't enjoy doing, but the truth is, I choose to spend my time in other ways. The same is true about putting God first. A friend that is always put last doesn't remain a friend for long. When it comes to God, we know he will never desert us, but what about our turning our backs on him? We know what we must do – put God first and then everything else falls into place. Even carrying the crosses each of us must bear in life is easier because we know we don't have to do it alone. Sometimes we may have to disappoint a child or friend because we choose to do the right thing, but that is the price of being a disciple of Jesus.

Prayer

Thank you Lord for the family and friends that I have, and I know that if I put you first in my life, my relationships with family and friends will be better because of it as I will be a more loving person. Amen.

Note   Date:

_____

_____

_____

_____

_____

_____

_____

_____

Monday

Text : Luke 10:36-37

Inspiration

Several years ago, I was in Copenhagen, Denmark on a remarkable vacation and heard a story that gives new meaning to the answer to this question. We have all heard of the atrocities of the holocaust and its tragedies, but I had never heard the remarkable story of this nation. There is a little fishing village which is a suburb of Copenhagen that opened its arms to the Danish Jews during this terrible time. The fishermen let it be known that if you showed up in the village at the appointed time you would be evacuated to safety. In this way, 95% of Danish Jews escaped deportation and execution. This in itself is enough to show their concern for their neighbors, but there was more.

After the war, when the people returned home to Denmark, they returned to their jobs, their homes, their properties which had been cared for and kept safe by their Christian neighbors. It made me consider how often I go out of my way for a friend, let alone others I may not know. It makes me ponder how well I live out the command to love my neighbor as myself. Would I have been as generous as the Danes under those extreme circumstances? Could I be that generous today? Do I know my neighbors well enough to tell when they might be in trouble? These are questions that I will ponder long after the pictures are looked at, the vacation stories have been told, the souvenirs given away. I hope that having the experiences I encountered on vacation will make me a better person, one who doesn't pass by, or look the other way, when a neighbor is in need.

Prayer

Lord I confess that I have not always been a good neighbor to those around me. Too often my priorities and preference have kept me from sharing your love. Give me eyes to see others through your love, so that I may be prepared to offer help where it is needed. In Jesus name amen.

Note   Date:

_____

_____

_____

_____

_____

_____

_____

_____

Tuesday

Topic : True Prophecy
Text : 2Peter 1:19-21

Inspiration

Peter is warning the people against false teachers and false prophets. There were false prophets among the Israelites and there would be again. Men, then, and men and women today who would lead people away from the will of God in order that they might exert influence over the leaders of the times to achieve their own ends. In ancient times, the prophets worked to bring the people back to living as God wanted them to live. The false prophets wanted to keep their jobs as the favorites of the kings and kept telling them not to listen.

Today we have many false teachers as Peter predicted who try to turn the words of Scripture to their own agendas. These people have often called for hate instead of the love which Jesus asked for. They have called for vengeance instead of forgiveness or mercy. They bring about division instead of unity. The true teacher will be attentive to the word of God and do his or her best to make Jesus law of love more visible in today's world.

These teachers are truly moved by the Holy Spirit and do not try to reinterpret Scripture, but to faithfully proclaim it.

Prayer

Lord, we, too, can fall into the trap of taking passages out of context to serve our own purposes. Please let us be guided by the holy spirit whenever we proclaim your word. Amen.

Note   Date:

_____

_____

_____

_____

_____

_____

_____

_____

_____

Wednesday

Topic : Forgiveness
Text : Genesis 45:4-5

Inspiration

Joseph is a lot more forgiving than I'm afraid I
would be. Joseph not only forgives his brothers but
sees God's hand in allowing their sin to bring good
out of evil. How do we look at sins committed
against us? Can we find any good that has come
from them? I can remember losing a job because of
the lies of a co-worker. It was devastating at the
time, and yet it led to my being able to live out one
of my childhood dreams and then to some of the
happiest years of my life. The co-worker lost her job
soon after. There are so many times when if we look
back we can see how God is working. We also can
see how a lack of forgiveness can cause damage to
families, communities and beyond. I've seen this
with divorce where one or both parents try to turn
their child against the other parent. This can
damage the child but also the parents themselves
and their families. Forgiveness might not be easy,
but ongoing hostility and anger can cause physical
as well as psychological damage. I'm sure you have
seen this among your friends if not in your own

family. We need to learn from Joseph. If we are having problems forgiving, we can ask God to help us. We ask God to forgive us, and he will also help us forgive others as he wants us to be free of the bonds that not forgiving keep us bound.

Prayer

Lord, we thank you for your willingness to forgive us. Please give us the graces we need to forgive this who have sinned against us. Amen.

Note   Date:

_____

_____

_____

_____

_____

_____

_____

_____

Thursday

Topic : Sin's punishment
Text : Genesis 42:21-22

Inspiration

People often blame God when bad things happen and feel it's God's punishment for sin But this passage from Genesis lets us know that sometimes sin brings its own punishment. We all know the story of Joseph and his coat of many colors that his brothers were so envious of since they were jealous of their father's preference for Joseph. We know how they sold their brother and told their father he was dead and how Joseph wound up in Egypt. Now the brothers are in Egypt seeking food because there was a famine in Canaan where they were living. Joseph recognizes them, but they don't have a clue. Now, they feel the guilt of having sold their brother and know that they deserve whatever happens to them. Sin has effects. People who lie aren't trusted. People who steal, find it hard to get a job. People who flaunt authority, who feel the rules don't apply to them, run into problems and often find themselves in jail. Many of these people will ask, "Why me? Why is God doing this to me?" The answer is obvious to others. God isn't doing anything to them, they have done it to themselves. The easy answer to avoiding these problems is just don't sin, but we know that that isn't always possible. What we can do is to take responsibility for our behavior, recognize our sins, ask for forgiveness and ask for help to avoid sin in the future.

Prayer

Forgiving Lord, you don't need to punish us as we seem to do a good job of doing that ourselves. Help us to recognize our sins and ask you for forgivenessas well as the strength to avoid the situations that leads us into sin. Amen.

Note   Date:

_____

_____

_____

_____

_____

_____

_____

_____

_____

_____

Friday

Topic : The Important Things
Text : Proverb 2:1-5

Inspiration

What is important to you? This proverb tells us
what is necessary if finding knowledge of God is
what we are searching for. When this is compared
to the search for silver or hidden treasures, we see
how diligently the search should be. What we need
to do first is to listen to God's word and to keep the
commandments. If we look for wisdom with an
understanding heart, we are on our way to finding
God. But it seems as if not all roads will lead to this
knowledge because we need discernment, we need
to judge whether we are following the right path
and with this comes understanding If we look
carefully at this passage what we find is basically
the Gifts of the Holy Spirit. The only things missing
are fortitude or courage, and reverence or piety. We
know today that these gifts are there for us if we
choose to ask the Spirit for them. They are there for
us from the moment of our baptism. These gifts are
there for more than just the knowledge of God, they
are there to help us throughout our lives. When we
need strength to do the right thing, when we want

to know what is the right thing to do, we can ask the Spirit for help. We need to remember that the Spirit is there willing and able to help us if only we ask.

Prayer

Lord, there are so many ways that you let us know that we are not alone. Helps us to remember to call on you in good times and in bad, to give you thanks and praise, and to ask for your guidance in the decisions we make. Amen.

Note   Date:

Saturday

Topic : My Refuge, My Fortress
Text : Psalm 91:1-2

Inspiration

 When we are in trouble, where do we turn? Is God our first thought? Do we really believe that God is our fortress, and our refuge? From the beginning Scripture tells us to trust in God. From Adam and Eve, we find human beings want to trust in themselves first. When we fail, then we turn to God. Ever wonder what it might be like to turn to God first? If we turn to God and place our trust in him, it would save us a lot of unnecessary anxiety. The key is trust. We need to trust that God knows best, that he is with us through whatever is going on, that our prayers are being heard. The difficulty is that we think we know what's best and we can get upset when God has other plans. We pray and don't like the answer, or don't want to wait for the answer.

I remember a story once told me about how we can miss God's answer because it wasn't the answer we wanted. A woman had to work to pay her bills and her mother got sick and needed full time care. She prayed and prayed that God would somehow take care of her problem. She couldn't continue to work and still be at home with her mother. Then her boss called her in and told her that business had slowed down and he needed to let her go temporarily but that she was such a good employee, he was willing to continue to pay her during this period. She went out of the office and complained to God that he had not answered her prayer but had made things worse. She never saw that she now had the money to pay her bills as well as the time her mother needed so that she could heal. God doesn't always do what we want, but he gives us what we need. When we put things in God's hands – and don't keep trying to take them back – we can relax knowing that all will be well.

Prayer

Lord, we say we trust in you but so often we get impatient and forget that you are always there at our side. Help us in our times of trial to hold on to that trust. Amen.

Note   Date:

_____

_____

_____

_____

_____

_____

_____

_____

_____

_____

Week 3

Sunday

Topic : Labourers are few
Text : Luke 10:2

Inspiration

When Jesus says that the harvest is abundant but the laborers are few, do you think he was only talking about his time here on earth, or was he talking about now as well? If statistics are correct, most people who identify themselves as Christian do not attend church on a regular basis. Where are the others? Where are the laborers who should be gathering the harvest? We need to pray for men and women to answer the call to minister to God's people but we also need to pray for ourselves to reach out to those who don't understand the value of what we have. Do you talk about the importance of your faith in God with others in your family, your circle of friends? I know that I was told as a child that the two things you don't talk about are religion and politics, but why?

Perhaps when people were refused jobs or housing on the basis of their religious beliefs, it was necessary, but today? If you are in the market for a car – or a computer – who would you talk to? If you only talk to professionals, you might think you're just getting a sales pitch, so you ask your friends or relatives what they own and whether or not they would recommend it. I'm not dismissing the value of those of us who are professionals in the faith department! But I am suggesting that each of us as friend and relative has more influence than we think. We understand how our faith gets us through the tough times. How we welcome the support of our community in times of joy as well as sorrow. We understand the value of faith in our lives. What makes us so afraid to talk about it? At this particular time in our churches and in our world, the need for laborers is great indeed. Will you go out into the fields?

Prayer

Lord, you have called us by our baptism to be your disciple. Give us the grace we need to go into the fields where you have sent us to preach your message of salvation. Amen

Note   Date:

Monday

Topic : You are a Temple of the Holy Spirit
Text : 1Corinthians 6:18-20

Inspiration

This is a hard saying in today's world. Sexual immorality is so rampant and public that few people believe it to be immoral! People no longer think of sexual behavior outside of marriage as wrong and, in fact, have no problem with going from one person to another quite publicly, broadcasting their behavior on social media and if you're famous enough, on twitter, on TV, in magazines, etc. What happened to "Thou shalt not commit adultery?" I guess I'm old fashioned. I'm not about to condemn anyone who truly loves another and is faithful to them regardless of marriage, but I don't understand and cannot condone random sexual encounters that are not based on love but lust, have no desire for permanency but are literally just to satisfy a sexual itch.

Sorry if I offend anyone, but if we believe that our bodies are temples of the Holy Spirit to be kept holy, how can we treat them as what – toys, prizes?

I'm aware that women have often been treated as sexual objects rather than human beings, but men have also been treated badly and often have been given expectations that are false. Men and women are all created in the same image of God with the same free will and with the same purpose, to be the face of God in the world. And our God is not like the promiscuous gods of the Romans, the Greeks, the Egyptians or any other culture. For our God is one of unconditional love, and as he loves us, he expects us to love others and that does not mean using another for pleasure. I hope that someday, we will cease to promote immorality and be more concerned with our immortality.

Prayer

Lord, we have come so far from the people we were created to be. Help us to return to you and live your commandments with a renewed respect for the body you have given us. Amen.

Note   Date:

_____

_____

_____

_____

_____

_____

_____

_____

Tuesday

Topic : Loss or Gain
Text : Philippians 3:8-11

Inspiration

Paul is telling us and the Philippians that whatever
he has suffered, whatever he has lost, it is nothing
compared to what he has gained in Christ.
Whenever we make changes in our lives, we lose as
well as gain. When we move on from high school to
the work force or to college, we will gain friends and
lose friends. If we change jobs, we may even lose
the ability to see our families as often as we had
been able to do. If we change our religion or our
religious habits, we also may lose friends or even
connections with our family members. Christianity
requires changes in our lifestyle if we are to be
faithful to God's will. Doing the right thing becomes
more important than hanging out with friends who
can lead you in a different direction. Attitudes can
change and your behavior with them. You're no
longer the fun person who likes the dirty jokes who
doesn't complain about foul language, who won't go
to the x-rated movies, or engage in other activities
contrary to Jesus' law of love. What is lost, however,
is so much greater, as Paul tells us. Faith gives us

trust in God's promises, freedom from fear of the future. We have been made acceptable to the Father through Christ.

Prayer

Lord, we have gained so much because of Christ. May we like Paul consider all we have lost as nothing and look only to what we have now through Faith. Amen.

Note   Date:

_____

_____

_____

_____

_____

_____

_____

_____

_____

Wednesday

Topic : Abraham's Sacrifice
Text : Genesis 22:11-12

Inspiration

Did you ever wonder what went through Abraham's mind when he believed that God wanted him to sacrifice his son? Of course, at that particular time in history, sacrifice of the first-born was not unusual and seen as an offering to the gods who would then allow the rest of the children to live. Did Abraham think that God was like the other gods? We will never know in this world. But God did not want sacrifice in the flesh, but sacrifice in the heart. Abraham was prevented from sacrificing Isaac and was given a ram instead, and for his willingness was promised great blessings. What are we willing to sacrifice for God?

Today, in America, we celebrate our independence. Many men and women sacrificed a great deal for this to happen and many people all over the world have sacrificed a great deal for their independence, independence from tyranny, independence to practice their religion, freedom from fear. Isaac was freed so that he could become the father of Esau and Jacob and thereby the grandfather of Israel. Jesus has freed us, has given us independence from the tyranny of law by giving us the law of love to follow. He has freed us so that we might experience the joys of eternal life. We all have much to celebrate today no matter where we live, so let us thank God for freedom.

Prayer

Loving God, you gave Abraham back his son and you give us so much. May we always be grateful for all your gift, and today especially, we thank you for the freedom of fear death and the gift of salvation. Amen.

Note   Date:

_____

_____

_____

_____

_____

_____

_____

_____

_____

Thursday

Topic : Let us bless the Lord
Text : Psalm 34:1-4

Inspiration

This is one of the psalms attributed to David. He is thanking God for rescuing him and promising to bless God at all times. He asks us to join him in his praises. He says his soul shall boast in the Lord. St. Paul tells us that we, too, should only boast in the Lord because it is he who always saves us. So, today, make a list. Make a list of everything that you are thankful for. Make a list of every success you have had and every failure you have survived. Make a list of every person who has helped you grow as a person and as a Christian. Now, look at it. Each of the items, events or persons on these lists are blessings from God. Either now, or before the day is over, bless and thank God for each of them. Ask God, also, to bless each of the people you have listed that you might be a blessing for them. If some of them are now with God, they would still like to hear you say thank you. God is so good to us all the time, and as one of my favorite people once answered, and all the time God is good.

Prayer

Heavenly Father, we thank you for all the times you have been there for us even when we were unaware of your presence. We thank you for the people you have sent to us to help us grow and we ask you to bless them in turn. Amen.

Note   Date:

_____

_____

_____

_____

_____

_____

_____

_____

_____

Friday

Topic : Lot's Rescue
Text : Genesis 19:15-16

Inspiration

When I read about Lot and the destruction of
Sodom and Gomorrah, I tend to think about Lot's
wife and her turning back just when salvation was
in her grasp. The angels had brought the whole
family to safety; all they had to do was follow God's
instruction not to turn back. It sounds so easy. I
wonder what was so important to Lot's wife that she
turned back? I'm sure that Lot was grateful to God
and to the angels for rescuing him and his family
and also saddened by the loss of his wife. We, too,
have been rescued. We have been rescued from the
fear of death, from the effects of our sinfulness and
from eternal damnation. We have chosen to follow
our deliverer, our Savior, Jesus Christ. What is
there in our lives that is so important to us that we
risk losing it all? Because we do turn back, just as
Lot's wife. We often return to old habits, old
companions that lead us into sinful situations, old
temptations that we think won't entrap us. We
choose to ignore what has been done for us.
Hopefully, we will have the sense to return to

Christ, ask forgiveness, and work at moving toward a new way of living instead of returning to the past.

Prayer

Forgiving and Compassionate God, how often we ignore your commandments and follow our own ways instead of the ways of your son, Jesus. Give us the graces we need to do your will. Amen.

Note   Date:

_____

_____

_____

_____

_____

_____

_____

_____

Saturday

Topic : Say Thank You
Text : Psalm 50:22-23

Inspiration

As small children we were all taught to say please and thank you, but as adults we sometimes forget. This psalm reminds us that we owe God a thank you for everything we have. Gratitude is so important but we often forget that it is God who provides us with what we need. When things go wrong, or when we want something, we have no problem asking God to intervene and provide us with what we want. We sometimes get upset with God when things don't go the way we wanted, when God says no or maybe later, but how often do we remember to say thanks? When things are going smoothly, we also can forget about God. Do we ever think that things going smoothly is a result of God's goodness? I try very hard to remember to say thanks every night before going to sleep. I find it a habit I have developed over the years thanks to my grandmother and if I forget, I wake up later as if she's prompting me from heaven! God is not going to strike me with lightening if I forget, but I know that my life is more peaceful when I remember. Gratitude is a habit we should all develop and it helps us recognize how much more we have than how much we lack. It helps us focus on the positive rather than the negative and that leads to a more joyous life. We all know that God has saved us, but do we also think about the small gifts he gives us each day? Let's always remember to say thank you.

Prayer

Lord, you give us so much. It's easy to think that the small victories we have each day are of our own doing but without you, we can do nothing. Thank you for your abiding presence. Amen.

Note   Date:

Week 4

Topic : To live in Christ
Text : Galatians 2:19-20

Inspiration

We know that we who have been baptized have been baptized into his death so that we might rise with him. The words may be a little different from those of Paul, but the message is the same, if we are willing to accept it. By accepting our baptism, we are choosing to live a life of faith, remembering the sacrifice of Jesus. It's a willingness to die to self, not easy. Of course, for Paul the dangers were more immediate, and for many Christians today, that hasn't changed. But some have said that it would be easier to die once for our faith than to have to die every day. I hope I never have to face that possibility, but having just written that, I think I do have to face that and we all do. We all will need to face death one day, whether or not it comes suddenly or after a lingering illness. We will have to face the reality of death. Will we be at peace, even joyous that we will be with our God? Or will we be fearful, our faith tested for a final time? This is Satan's last chance to get to us. Hopefully, by dying with Christ in spirit, and living in him, our faith will be strong when it is time to die with Christ in the flesh.

Prayer

Loving God, we have willingly been baptized in the death of your son Jesus. Help us live in him so that we will be ready to meet him at the end of our earthly lives. Amen.

Note   Date:

_____

_____

_____

_____

_____

_____

_____

_____

Monday

Topic : Turn to Me
Text : Joel 2:12-13

Inspiration

Again we have a prophet spreading God's message of love, begging the people to admit their wrongdoing, and sincerely repent and turn back to him. When you read the Old Testament, you start to wonder if they will ever learn. I wonder what historians one hundred years from now will say about us and our behavior. Will they read the New Testament and find remnants of Christian groups and compare their behavior with the Bible, and find us worthy of the name? I'm not so sure. Not only is there a lot of what I consider very un-Christian behavior by individuals but also by Christian groups towards one another. Perhaps we should reread Joel and the messages given by some of the other prophets and take these messages to heart. God wants us to turn to him. He wants us to take responsibility for our actions, and ask forgiveness so that he can forgive and renew us. God isn't looking for grandiose exhibitions of repentance, but a sincerity of heart. It's how much we are willing to change our behavior. It's how welcoming we will be to the stranger, how much we are willing to help others to grow in their faith as well as how willing we are to grow in our own.

Prayer

Forgiving God, you are so patient with us, we repeat our sinful behavior again and again. We turn to you today and ask for your forgiveness and the desire to change. Amen.

Note   Date:

_____

_____

_____

_____

_____

_____

_____

_____

Tuesday

Topic : Beware of false prophets
Text : Matthew 7:15-17

Inspiration

We need to be on the lookout for those who would
lead people away from God by pretending that they
are leading them to God. We have seen this happen
several times in very public and tragic ways, but it
can happen in less public ways as well. The world
was horrified when they learned of the mass
murder/suicide of over 900 people, one third of
them minors in Guyana in 1978, and again of the
destruction of the compound in Waco, Texas where
over 70 people died. Both of these tragedies
occurred because the leaders of the cult claimed to
either be a god or be God's messenger or Messiah.
There have been many other cults operating with
less destructive results. Preying on loners or
immigrants, the leaders promise security here and
eternal life if only you follow them. They don't say
that you are following God, but you are following
them because they are the only ones who know the
way! By their fruits you will know them. These
people ask blind obedience, work to separate people
from their families and friends, and often demand a

certain percentage of income. This doesn't sound like Jesus to me. Paul never demanded obedience to himself, in fact, he said just the opposite to the Corinthians. John the Baptist said that he wasn't the one and pointed to Jesus. We have been warned by Jesus to look at those who claim to be prophets carefully and judge by their fruits. If they are more interested in leading us to themselves instead of to Jesus, we must beware.

Prayer

Lord, you do send prophet in every age to help us know how to live in that age. Help us to know who is from you and who is not. Guide us to your truth. Amen.

Note   Date:

_____

_____

_____

_____

_____

_____

_____

_____

_____

Wednesday

Topic : God knows the path we should follow
Text : Genesis 12:1-3

Inspiration

I'm not sure that I would have had the courage to do what Abram did. Where did he find the faith to listen to this voice of God and believe? Abram was not a nomad, he lived in a land that he knew. He had a family with responsibilities. But he went, and his nephew went with him and his wife and their animals and herdsmen. They didn't have a clue where they were headed, but believed. They trusted a God they hadn't yet come to know. We have had over 4000 years of Scripture to read and reflect upon, and we still have problems trusting that God knows the path we should be following. We stumble around as in the dark, when we have the light of the Gospel to guide us. Because of Abram's willingness to follow God, he is the Father in Faith for three of the major religions in today's world. God doesn't ask us to venture into the unknown as he did Abram, he has given us a way to follow by sending Jesus to go before us. By following him and living as he lived, we, too, will be blessed. Through Abram, later Abraham, we have come to know the one God who cares for us and has blessed us because of his faith by sending us our Messiah.

Prayer

Heavenly Father, you called Abram your servant, who left his home and follow where you led. Give us that same faith to follow you and live as you would have us live. Amen.

Note   Date:

_____

_____

_____

_____

_____

_____

_____

_____

_____

Thursday

Topic :. Who Do You Say That I Am?
Text : Luke 9:18-20

Inspiration

This is one of my favorite Gospel Passages. It's a
question that I have often used for meditation both
for myself and for classes I have taught to both
teens and adults. It's a question that I think we
need to reflect upon often as we can lose sight of the
importance of Jesus in our lives. And the answer
can change. He might be friend, brother, Lord,
Savior, shepherd, leader, companion – or just
someone we have heard about. One teen answered
the question by saying that Jesus was a nice man. Is
that all he is? What about the Son of God – Divine?
Does it make a difference in my life if I believe that
Jesus is God, the Second Person of the Blessed
Trinity who came to save me from eternal death by
his dying on a cross? Does it make a difference in
how I live if I believe that this is not the end? This is
a time for getting to know him better so that I can
also live eternally in heaven with the Father. I know
this because of the resurrection. Yes, Jesus can be
my friend and companion, but he is so much more
than that. By his life, I know how to live. By his

dying and rising, I can face my own death and the death of those I love because he has shown me that this is not the end. In this today's gospel, Jesus tell us that we must pick up our cross and follow him. Are we willing to deny ourselves in order to follow Jesus? What am I being asked to change in my life, right now? I am so glad that we are reminded each we read this question that Jesus asks – not just the disciples – but us as well. Who do I say that Jesus is for me, today?

Prayer

Loving God, you sent us your son to save us. May we come to know him better in all his fullness of Divinity and his Humanity. Amen.

Note   Date:

_____

_____

_____

_____

_____

_____

_____

_____

Friday

Topic : They Didn't Listen
Text : 2Chronicles 24:17-19

Inspiration

Time and time again, prophets were sent to the
leaders of Israel trying to bring them back to God,
away from their idols, but they didn't listen. The
time described above is not different and the result
is not different. The leaders wanted the king to rule
in their favor, they wanted power, and whatever
else they could get. What they got, however, was the
Syrian army that came to Judah and Jerusalem and
destroyed all the princes of the people that had
gone against God and sent the spoils to Damascus.
What did they gain by worshiping idols? What do
we gain by ignoring the teachings of Jesus and
making idols of money, power, fame, and even
ourselves? People with too much money often live
in fear that someone will come and steal it. Notice
that the fences and walls of the rich are usually
higher than those of the poor. Fame is fleeting and
those who have it spend a lot of time worrying
about their safety. Power? There's always someone
who wants to take their place and are willing to do
almost anything to get it. There's no point in talking

about those who put themselves up as some kind of god as they may achieve all of the above – fame, power, and money – but their lifestyles usually are missing something very important, happiness. The people of Judah didn't find happiness by ignoring God, and neither will we.

Prayer

Gracious God, may we have ears open to hear your message of love and your rules for achieving true happiness and the will to follow you. Amen.

Note   Date:

Saturday

Topic : Don't Be A Show Off
Text : Matthew 6:1-2

Inspiration

Many people do good things. The question here is, why? One summer I worked in the office of a major university where I recorded the donations that came in on cards with the name of the donor on them. I came across many names of prominent people who were quite familiar to me, but there was a notation on the top of many of those cards that said "anonymous." Many of these people actually had two cards, one for the public and the other not. The public one was for far less money. They wanted to support the college, but didn't want credit for their generosity. Obviously, people will be rewarded here for a generosity of spirit, they will be known for performing acts of heroism. We know the names of people who have worked to spread the gospel message and those who work tirelessly for justice. This does not take away from their sacrifice. But, there also are people who want to be known for their good acts and it is these that Jesus warns about. It is one thing for people to come to know the goodness of others; it is another for that person to call attention to what they are doing for their own glory. Do we act because as followers of Christ we are called to do what we do? Or, do we want attention?

Prayer

Lord, may I always do the right thing for the right reasons. Loving your people and working for justice should not be done for the glory of anyone except you. Amen.

Note   Date:

_____

_____

_____

_____

_____

_____

_____

_____